SRI AUROBINDO

AND

HIS ASHRAM

SRI AUROBINDO ASHRAM

PONDICHERRY

First edition: 1948
Sixth edition: 1983
Reprinted: 1987, 1990, 1993, 1995, 1997, 2000

ISBN 81-7058-221-0

Published by Sri Aurobindo Ashram Publication Department
Printed at All India Press, Pondicherry – 605 001
PRINTED IN INDIA

Publisher's Note

For some time past there has been a growing demand, both in India and abroad, to know more about Sri Aurobindo, the Mother, their Ashram, and their teaching. This book is an attempt, in brief compass, to meet this demand.

Some of the material printed here was written by Sri Aurobindo himself. He wrote (in the third person) the article "Political Life" after certain inauthentic reports had come out in the press. "The Fifteenth of August 1947" was written for broadcast on that date, India's Independence Day. He wrote "The Teaching of Sri Aurobindo" in 1934 as part of a booklet entitled *The Teaching and the Ashram of Sri Aurobindo*.

The section headed "Sri Aurobindo", written by one or more of his disciples, was seen and corrected by Sri Aurobindo before being published in 1937 as *Sri Aurobindo: A Life Sketch*.

The other material in this book was written by the editors. They have based themselves on the writings of Sri Aurobindo and the Mother and on other authentic sources. Wherever possible they have utilised quotations from these works.

CONTENTS

I

SRI AUROBINDO

Sri Aurobindo was born in Calcutta on 15 August 1872. In 1879, at the age of seven, he was taken with his two elder brothers to England for education and lived there for fourteen years. Brought up at first in an English family at Manchester, he joined St. Paul's School in London in 1884 and in 1890 went from it with a senior classical scholarship to King's College, Cambridge, where he studied for two years. In 1890 he passed also the open competition for the Indian Civil Service, but at the end of two years of probation failed to present himself at the riding examination and was disqualified for the Service. At this time the Gaekwar of Baroda was in London. Aurobindo saw him, obtained an appointment in the Baroda Service and left England for India in January 1893.

Sri Aurobindo passed thirteen years, from 1893 to 1906, in the Baroda Service, first in the Revenue Department and in secretariate work for the Maharaja, afterwards as Professor of English and, finally, Vice-Principal in the Baroda College. These were years of self-culture, of literary activity – for much of the poetry afterwards published from Pondicherry was written at this time – and of preparation for his future work. In England he had received, according to his father's express instructions, an entirely occidental education without any contact with the culture of India and the East.* At Baroda he made up the deficiency, learned Sanskrit and several modern Indian languages, assimilated the spirit of Indian civilisation and its forms past and present. A great part of the last years of this period was spent on leave in silent political activity, for he was debarred from public action by his position at Baroda. The outbreak of the agitation against the partition of Bengal in 1905 gave him the opportunity to give up the Baroda Service and join openly in the political move-

* It may be observed that Sri Aurobindo's education in England gave him a wide introduction to the culture of ancient, of mediaeval and of modern Europe. He was a brilliant scholar in Greek and Latin. He had learned French from his childhood in Manchester and studied for himself German and Italian sufficiently to study Goethe and Dante in the original tongues. (He passed the Tripos in Cambridge in the first class and obtained record marks in Greek and Latin in the examination for the Indian Civil Service.)

ment. He left Baroda in 1906 and went to Calcutta as Principal of the newly-founded Bengal National College.

The political action of Sri Aurobindo covered eight years, from 1902 to 1910. During the first half of this period he worked behind the scenes, preparing with other co-workers the beginnings of the Swadeshi (Indian Sinn Fein) movement, till the agitation in Bengal furnished an opening for the public initiation of a more forward and direct political action than the moderate reformism which had till then been the creed of the Indian National Congress. In 1906 Sri Aurobindo came to Bengal with this purpose and joined the New Party, an advanced section small in numbers and not yet strong in influence, which had been recently formed in the Congress. The political theory of this party was a rather vague gospel of Non-cooperation; in action it had not yet gone farther than some ineffective clashes with the Moderate leaders at the annual Congress assembly behind the veil of secrecy of the "Subjects Committee". Sri Aurobindo persuaded its chiefs in Bengal to come forward publicly as an All-India party with a definite and challenging programme, putting forward Tilak, the popular Maratha leader at its head, and to attack the then dominant Moderate (Reformist or Liberal) oligarchy of veteran politicians and capture from them the Congress and the country. This was the origin of the historic struggle between the Moderates and the Nationalists (called by their opponents Extremists) which in two years changed altogether the face of Indian politics.

The new-born Nationalist party put forward Swaraj (independence) as its goal as against the far-off Moderate hope of colonial self-government to be realised at a distant date of a century or two by a slow progress of reform; it proposed as its means of execution a programme which resembled in spirit, though not in its details, the policy of Sinn Fein developed some years later and carried to a successful issue in Ireland. The principle of this new policy was self-help; it aimed on one side at an effective organisation of the forces of the nation and on the other professed a complete non-cooperation with the Government. Boycott of British and foreign goods and the fostering of Swadeshi industries to replace them, boycott of British law courts and the foundation of a system of Arbitration courts in their stead, boycott of Government universities and colleges and the creation of a network of National colleges and schools, the formation of societies of young men which would do the work of police and defence and, wherever necessary, a policy of passive resistance were among the immediate items of the programme. Sri Aurobindo hoped to capture the Congress and make it the directing centre of an organised national action, an informal State within the State, which would carry on the struggle for freedom till it was won. He persuaded the party to take up and finance as its recognised organ the newly-founded daily paper, *Bande Mataram*, of which he was at the time acting editor. The *Bande Mataram*, whose policy from the beginning of 1907 till its abrupt winding up in 1908 when Sri Aurobindo was in prison was wholly directed by him, circulated almost immediately all over India. During its brief but momentous existence it changed the political thought of India which has ever since preserved fundamentally, even amidst its later developments, the stamp then imparted to it. But the struggle initiated on these lines, though vehement and eventful and full of importance for the future, did not last long at the time; for the country was still unripe for so bold a programme.

Sri Aurobindo was prosecuted for sedition in 1907 and acquitted. Up till now an organiser and writer, he was obliged by this event and by the imprisonment or disappearance of other leaders to come forward as the acknowledged head of the party in Bengal and to appear on the platform for the first time as a speaker. He presided over the Nationalist Conference at Surat in 1907 where in the forceful clash of two equal parties the Congress was broken to pieces. In May, 1908 he was arrested in the Alipur Conspiracy Case as implicated in the doings of the revolutionary group led by his brother Barindra; but no evidence of any value could be established against him and in this case too he was acquitted. After a detention of one year as undertrial prisoner in the Alipur Jail, he came out in May 1909, to find the party organisation broken, its leaders scattered by imprisonment, deportation or self-imposed exile and the party itself still existent but dumb and dispirited and incapable of any strenuous action. For almost a year he strove single-handed as the sole remaining leader of the Nationalists in India to revive the movement. He published at this time to aid his effort a weekly English paper, the *Karmayogin*, and a Bengali weekly, the *Dharma*. But at last he was compelled to recognise that the nation was not yet sufficiently trained to carry out his policy and programme. For a time he thought that the necessary training must first be given through a less advanced Home Rule movement or an agitation of passive resistance of the kind created by Mahatma Gandhi in South Africa. But he saw that the hour of these movements had not come and that he himself was not their destined leader. Moreover, since his twelve months' detention in the Alipur Jail, which had been spent entirely in practice of Yoga, his inner spiritual life was pressing upon him for an exclusive concentration. He resolved therefore to withdraw from the political field, at least for a time.

In February 1910, he withdrew to a secret retirement at Chandernagore and in the beginning of April sailed for Pondicherry in French India. A third prosecution was launched against him at this moment for a signed article in the *Karmayogin*; in his absence it was pressed against the printer of the paper who was convicted, but the conviction was quashed on appeal in the High Court of Calcutta. For the third time a prosecution against him had failed. Sri Aurobindo had left Bengal with some intention of returning to the political field under more favourable circumstances; but very soon the magnitude of the spiritual work he had taken up appeared to him and he saw that it would need the exclusive concentration of all his energies. Eventually he cut off connection with politics, refused repeatedly to accept the Presidentship of the National Congress and went into a complete retirement. During all his stay at Pondicherry from 1910 onward he remained more and more exclusively devoted to his spiritual work and his sadhana.

In 1914 after four years of silent Yoga he began the publication of a philosophical monthly, the *Arya*. Most of his more important works, *The Life Divine, The Synthesis of Yoga, Essays on the Gita, The Isha Upanishad,* appeared serially in the *Arya*. These works embodied much of the inner knowledge that had come to him in his practice of Yoga. Others were concerned with the spirit and significance of Indian civilisation and culture (*The Foundations of Indian Culture*), the true meaning of the Vedas (*The Secret of the Veda*), the progress of human society (*The Human Cycle*), the nature and evolution of poetry (*The Future Poetry*), the possibility of the unification of the human race (*The Ideal of Human Unity*). At this time also he began to publish his poems, both those written in England and at

Baroda and those, fewer in number, added during his period of political activity and in the first years of his residence at Pondicherry. The *Arya* ceased publication in 1921 after six years and a half of uninterrupted appearance.

Sri Aurobindo lived at first in retirement at Pondicherry with four or five disciples. Afterwards more and yet more began to come to him to follow his spiritual path and the number became so large that a community of sadhaks had to be formed for the maintenance and collective guidance of those who had left everything behind for the sake of a higher life. This was the foundation of the Sri Aurobindo Ashram which has less been created than grown around him as its centre.

Sri Aurobindo began his practice of Yoga in 1904. At first gathering into it the essential elements of spiritual experience that are gained by the paths of divine communion and spiritual realisation followed till now in India, he passed on in search of a more complete experience uniting and harmonising the two ends of existence, Spirit and Matter. Most ways of Yoga are paths to the Beyond leading to the Spirit and, in the end, away from life; Sri Aurobindo's rises to the Spirit to redescend with its gains bringing the light and power and bliss of the Spirit into life to transform it. Man's present existence in the material world is in this view or vision of things a life in the Ignorance with the Inconscient at its base, but even in its darkness and nescience there are involved the presence and possibilities of the Divine. The created world is not a mistake or a vanity and illusion to be cast aside by the soul returning to heaven or Nirvana, but the scene of a spiritual evolution by which out of this material inconscience is to be manifested progressively the Divine Consciousness in things. Mind is the highest term yet reached in the evolution, but it is not the highest of which it is capable. There is above it a Supermind or eternal Truth-Consciousness which is in its nature the self-aware and self-determining light and power of a Divine Knowledge. Mind is an ignorance seeking after Truth, but this is a self-existent Knowledge harmoniously manifesting the play of its forms and forces. It is only by the descent of this Supermind that the perfection dreamed of by all that is highest in humanity can come. It is possible by opening to a greater Divine Consciousness to rise to this power of light and bliss, discover one's true self, remain in constant union with the Divine and bring down the supramental Force for the transformation of mind and life and body. To realise this possibility has been the dynamic aim of Sri Aurobindo's Yoga.

*

Sri Aurobindo left his body on 5 December 1950.

II

POLITICAL LIFE

There were three sides to Sri Aurobindo's political ideas and activities. First, there was the action with which he started, a secret revolutionary propaganda and organisation of which the central object was the preparation of an armed insurrection. Secondly, there was a public propaganda intended to convert the whole nation to the ideal of independence which was regarded, when he entered into politics, by the vast majority of Indians as unpractical and impossible, an almost insane chimera. It was thought that the British Empire was too powerful and India too weak, effectively disarmed and impotent even to dream of the success of such an endeavour. Thirdly, there was the organisation of the people to carry on a public and united opposition and undermining of the foreign rule through an increasing non-cooperation and passive resistance.

At that time the military organisation of the great empires and their means of military action were not so overwhelming and apparently irresistible as they now are: the rifle was still the decisive weapon, air power had not yet been developed and the force of artillery was not so devastating as it afterwards became. India was disarmed, but Sri Aurobindo thought that with proper organisation and help from outside this difficulty might be overcome and in so vast a country as India and with the smallness of the regular British armies, even a guerrilla warfare accompanied by general resistance and revolt might be effective. There was also the possibility of a general revolt in the Indian army. At the same time he had studied the temperament and characteristics of the British people and the turn of their political instincts, and he believed that although they would resist any attempt at self-liberation by the Indian people and would at the most only concede very slowly such reforms as would not weaken their imperial control, still they were not of the kind which would be ruthlessly adamantine to the end: if they found resistance and revolt becoming general and persistent they would in the end try to arrive at an accommodation to save what they could of their empire or in an extremity prefer to grant independence rather than have it forcefully wrested from their hands.

In some quarters there is the idea that Sri Aurobindo's political standpoint was entirely pacifist, that he was opposed in principle and in practice to all violence and that he denounced terrorism, insurrection, etc. as entirely forbidden by the spirit and letter of the Hindu religion. It is even suggested that he was a forerunner of the gospel of Ahimsa. This is quite incorrect. Sri Aurobindo is neither an impotent moralist nor a weak pacifist.

The rule of confining political action to passive resistance was adopted as the best policy for the National Movement at that stage and not as a part of a gospel of Non-violence or pacific idealism. Peace is a part of the highest ideal, but it must be spiritual or at the very least psychological in its basis; without a change in human nature it cannot come with any finality. If it is attempted on any other basis (moral principle or gospel of Ahimsa or any other), it will fail and even may leave things worse than before. He is in favour of an attempt to put down war by international agreement and international force, what is now contemplated in the "New Order", if that proves possible, but that would not be Ahimsa, it would be a putting down of anarchic force by legal force and even then one cannot be sure that it would be permanent. Within nations this sort of peace has been secured, but it does not prevent occasional civil wars and revolutions and political outbreaks and repressions, sometimes of a sanguinary character. The same might happen to a similar world-peace. Sri Aurobindo has never concealed his opinion that a nation is entitled to attain its freedom by violence, if it can do so or if there is no other way; whether it should do so or not, depends on what is the best policy, not on ethical considerations. Sri Aurobindo's position and practice in this matter was the same as Tilak's and that of other Nationalist leaders who were by no means Pacifists or worshippers of Ahimsa.

For the first few years in India, Sri Aurobindo abstained from any political activity (except the writing of the articles in the *Induprakash*) and studied the conditions in the country so that he might be able to judge more maturely what could be done. Then he made his first move when he sent a young Bengali soldier of the Baroda army, Jatin Banerji, as his lieutenant to Bengal with a programme of preparation and action which he thought might occupy a period of 30 years before fruition could become possible. As a matter of fact it has taken 50 years for the movement of liberation to arrive at fruition and the beginning of complete success. The idea was to establish secretly or, as far as visible action could be taken, under various pretexts and covers, revolutionary propaganda and recruiting throughout Bengal. This was to be done among the youth of the country while sympathy and support and financial and other assistance were to be obtained from the older men who had advanced views or could be won over to them. Centres were to be established in every town and eventually in every village. Societies of young men were to be established with various ostensible objects, cultural, intellectual or moral and those already existing were to be won over for revolutionary use. Young men were to be trained in activities which might be helpful for ultimate military action, such as riding, physical training, athletics of various kinds, drill and organised movement. As soon as the idea was sown it attained a rapid prosperity; already existing small groups and associations of young men who had not yet the clear idea or any settled programme of revolution began to turn in this direction and a few who had already the revolutionary aim were contacted and soon developed activity on organised lines; the few rapidly became many. Meanwhile Sri Aurobindo had met a member of the Secret Society in Western India, and taken the oath of the Society and had been introduced to the Council in Bombay. His future action was not pursued under any directions by this Council, but he took up on his own responsibility the task of generalising support for its objects in Bengal where as yet it had no membership or following. He spoke of the Society and its aim to P. Mitter and other leading men of the revolutionary group in Bengal and they took the oath of the Society and agreed to carry out its objects on the lines suggested by Sri Aurobindo. The special cover used by Mitter's group was association for lathi play which had already been popularised to some extent by Sarala Ghosal in Bengal among the young men; but other groups used other ostensible covers. Sri Aurobindo's attempt at a close organisation of the whole movement did not succeed, but the movement itself did not suffer by that, for the general idea was taken up and activity of many separate groups led to a greater and more widespread diffusion of the revolutionary drive and its action. Afterwards there came the partition of Bengal and a general outburst of revolt which favoured the rise of the extremist party and the great nationalist movement. Sri Aurobindo's activities were then turned more and more in this direction and the secret action became a secondary and subordinate element. He took advantage, however, of the Swadeshi movement to popularise the idea of violent revolt in the future. At Barin's suggestion he agreed to the starting of a paper, *Yugantar*, which was to preach open revolt and the absolute denial of the British rule and include such items as a series of articles containing instructions for Guerrilla warfare. Sri Aurobindo himself wrote some of the opening articles in the early numbers and he always exercised a general control; when a member of the sub-editorial staff, Swami Vivekananda's brother, presented himself on his own motion to the police in a search as the editor of the paper and was prosecuted, the *Yugantar* under Sri Aurobindo's orders adopted the policy of refusing to defend itself in a British Court on the ground that it did not recognise the foreign Government and this immensely increased the prestige and influence of the paper. It had as its chief writers and directors three of the ablest younger writers in Bengal, and it at once acquired an immense influence throughout Bengal. It may be noted that the Secret Society did not include terrorism in its programme but this element grew up in Bengal as a result of the strong repression and the reaction to it in that Province.

The public activity of Sri Aurobindo began with the writing of the articles in the *Induprakash*. These seven articles written at the instance of K.G. Deshpande, editor of the paper, and Sri Aurobindo's Cambridge friend, under the caption, 'New Lamps for Old' vehemently denounced the then Congress policy of pray, petition and protest and called for a dynamic leadership based upon self-help and fearlessness. But this outspoken and irrefutable criticism was checked by the action of a Moderate leader who frightened the editor and thus prevented any full development of his ideas in the paper; he had to turn aside to generalities such as the necessity of extending the activities of the Congress beyond the circle of the bourgeois or middle class and calling into it the masses. Finally, Sri Aurobindo suspended all public activity of this kind and worked only in secret till 1905, but he contacted Tilak whom he regarded as the one possible leader for a revolutionary party and met him at the Ahmedabad

Congress; there Tilak took him out of the pandal and talked to him for an hour in the grounds expressing his contempt for the Reformist movement and explaining his own line of action in Maharashtra.

Sri Aurobindo included in the scope of his revolutionary work one kind of activity which afterwards became an important item in the public programme of the Nationalist party. He encouraged the young men in the centres of work to propagate the Swadeshi idea which at that time was only in its infancy and hardly more than a fad of the few. One of the ablest men in these revolutionary groups was a Maratha named Sakharam Ganesh Deuskar who was an able writer in Bengali (his family had been long domiciled in Bengal) and who had written a popular life of Shivaji in Bengali in which he first brought in the name of Swaraj afterwards adopted by the Nationalists as their word for independence, – Swaraj became one item of the fourfold Nationalist programme. He published a book entitled *Desher Katha* describing in exhaustive detail the British commercial and industrial exploitation of India. This book had an immense repercussion in Bengal, captured the mind of young Bengal and assisted more than anything else in the preparation of the Swadeshi movement. Sri Aurobindo himself had always considered the shaking off of this economic yoke and the development of Indian trade and industry as a necessary concomitant of the revolutionary endeavour.

As long as he was in the Baroda service, Sri Aurobindo could not take part publicly in politics. Apart from that, he preferred to remain and act and even to lead from behind the scenes without his name being known in public; it was the Government's action in prosecuting him as editor of the *Bande Mataram* that forced him into public view. And from that time forward he became openly, what he had been for sometime already, a prominent leader of the Nationalist party, its principal leader in action in Bengal and the organiser there of its policy and strategy. He had decided in his mind the lines on which he wanted the country's action to run: what he planned was very much the same as was developed afterwards in Ireland as the Sinn Fein movement; but Sri Aurobindo did not derive his ideas, as some have represented, from Ireland, for the Irish movement became prominent later and he knew nothing of it till after he had withdrawn to Pondicherry. There was, moreover, a capital difference between India and Ireland which made his work much more difficult, for all its past history had accustomed the Irish people to rebellion against British rule and this history might be even described as a constant struggle for independence intermittent in its action but permanently there in principle; there was nothing of this kind in India. Sri Aurobindo had to establish and generalise the idea of independence in the mind of the Indian people and at the same time to push first a party and then the whole nation into an intense and organised political activity which would lead to the accomplishment of that ideal. His idea was to capture the Congress and to make it an instrument for revolutionary action instead of a centre of a timid constitutional agitation which would only talk and pass resolutions and recommendations to the foreign Government; if the Congress could not be captured, then a central revolutionary body would have to be created which could do this work. It was to be a sort of State within the State giving its directions to the people and creating organised bodies and institutions which would be its means of action; there must be an increasing non-cooperation and passive resistance which would render the administration of the country by a foreign Government difficult or finally impossible, a universal unrest which would wear down repression and finally, if need be, an open revolt all over the country. This plan included a boycott of British trade, the substitution of national schools for the Government institutions, the creation of arbitration courts to which the people could resort instead of depending on the ordinary courts of law, the creation of volunteer forces which would be the nucleus of an army of open revolt, and all other action that could make the programme complete. The part Sri Aurobindo took publicly in Indian politics was of brief duration, for he turned aside from it in 1910 and withdrew to Pondicherry; much of his programme lapsed in his absence, but enough had been done to change the whole face of Indian politics and the whole spirit of the Indian people, to make independence its aim and non-cooperation and resistance its method, and even an imperfect application of this policy heightening into sporadic periods of revolt has been sufficient to bring about the victory. The course of subsequent events followed largely the line of Sri Aurobindo's idea. The Congress was finally captured by the Nationalist party, declared independence its aim, organised itself for action, took almost the whole nation minus a majority of the Mohammedans and a minority of the depressed classes into acceptance of its leadership and eventually formed the first national Government in India and secured from Britain acceptance of independence for India.

At first Sri Aurobindo took part in Congress politics only from behind the scenes, as he had not yet decided to leave the Baroda Service; but he took long leave without pay in which, besides carrying on personally the secret revolutionary work, he attended the Barisal Conference broken up by the police and toured East Bengal along with Bepin Pal and associated himself closely with the forward group in the Congress. It was during this period that he joined Bepin Pal in the editing of the *Bande Mataram*, founded the new political party in Bengal and attended the Congress session at Calcutta at which the Extremists, though still a minority, succeeded under the leadership of Tilak in imposing part of their political programme on the Congress. The founding of the Bengal National College gave him the opportunity he needed and enabled him to resign his position in the Baroda Service and join the college as its Principal. Subodh Mullick, one of Sri Aurobindo's collaborators in his secret action and afterwards also in Congress politics, in whose house he usually lived when he was in Calcutta, had given a lakh of rupees for this foundation and had stipulated that Sri Aurobindo should be given a post of professor in the college with a salary of Rs. 150; so he was now free to give his whole time to the service of the country. Bepin Pal, who had been long expounding a policy of self-help and non-cooperation in his weekly journal, now started a daily with the name of *Bande Mataram*, but it was likely to be a brief adventure since he began with only Rs. 500 in his pocket and no firm assurance of financial assistance in the future. He asked Sri Aurobindo to join him in this venture to which a ready consent was given, for now Sri Aurobindo saw his opportunity for starting the public propaganda necessary for his revolutionary purpose. He called a meeting of the forward group of young men in the Congress and decided then to organise themselves openly as a new political party joining hands with the corresponding group in Maharashtra under the proclaimed leadership of Tilak and to join battle with the Moderate party which was done at the Calcutta session. He also persuaded them to take up the *Bande Mataram* daily as their party organ and a Bande Mataram Company was started to finance the paper, whose direction

Sri Aurobindo undertook during the absence of Bepin Pal who was sent on a tour in the districts to proclaim the purpose and programme of the new party. The new party was at once successful and the *Bande Mataram* paper began to circulate throughout India. On its staff were not only Bepin Pal and Sri Aurobindo but some other very able writers, Shyam Sundar Chakravarty, Hemendra Prasad Ghose and Bejoy Chatterjee. Shyam Sundar and Bejoy were masters of the English language, each with a style of his own; Shyam Sundar caught up something like Sri Aurobindo's way of writing and later on many took his articles for Sri Aurobindo's. But after a time dissensions arose between Bepin Pal on one side and the other contributors and the directors of the Company because of temperamental incompatibility and differences of political view especially with regard to the secret revolutionary action with which others sympathised but to which Bepin Pal was opposed. This ended soon in Bepin Pal's separation from the journal. Sri Aurobindo would not have consented to this departure, for he regarded the qualities of Pal as a great asset to the *Bande Mataram*, since Pal, though not a man of action or capable of political leadership, was perhaps the best and most original political thinker in the country, an excellent writer and a magnificent orator: but the separation was effected behind Sri Aurobindo's back when he was convalescing from a dangerous attack of fever. His name was even announced without his consent in *Bande Mataram* as editor but for one day only, as he immediately put a stop to it since he was still formally in the Baroda Service and in no way eager to have his name brought forward in public. Henceforward, however, he controlled the policy of the *Bande Mataram* along with that of the party in Bengal. Bepin Pal had stated the aim of the new party as complete self-government free from British control; but this could have meant or at least included the Moderate aim of colonial self-government and Dadabhai Naoroji as President of the Calcutta session of the Congress had actually tried to capture the name of Swaraj, the Extremists' term for independence, for this colonial self-government. Sri Aurobindo's first preoccupation was to declare openly for complete and absolute independence as the aim of political action in India and to insist on this persistently in the pages of the journal; he was the first politician in India who had the courage to do this in public and he was immediately successful. The party took up the word Swaraj to express its own ideal of independence and it soon spread everywhere; but it was taken up as the ideal of the Congress much later on at the Karachi session of that body when it had been reconstituted and renovated under Nationalist leadership. The journal declared and developed a new political programme for the country as the programme of the Nationalist party, non-cooperation, passive resistance, Swadeshi, Boycott, national education, settlement of disputes in law by popular arbitration and other items of Sri Aurobindo's plan. Sri Aurobindo published in the paper a series of articles on passive resistance, another developing a political philosophy of revolution and wrote many leaders aimed at destroying the shibboleths and superstitions of the Moderate Party, such as the belief in British justice and benefits bestowed by foreign government in India, faith in British law courts and in the adequacy of the education given in schools and universities in India and stressed more strongly and persistently than had been done the emasculation, stagnation or slow progress, poverty, economic dependence, absence of a rich industrial activity and all other evil results of a foreign government; he insisted especially that even if an alien rule were benevolent and beneficent, that could not be a substitute for a free and healthy national life. Assisted by this publicity the ideas of the Nationalists gained ground everywhere, especially in the Punjab which had before been predominantly moderate. The *Bande Mataram* was almost unique in journalistic history in the influence it exercised in converting the mind of a people and preparing it for revolution. But its weakness was on the financial side; for the Extremists were still a poor man's party. So long as Sri Aurobindo was there in active control, he managed with great difficulty to secure sufficient public support for running the paper, but not for expanding it as he wanted, and when he was arrested and held in jail for a year, the economic situation of *Bande Mataram* became desperate: finally, it was decided that the journal should die a glorious death rather than perish by starvation and Bejoy Chatterji was commissioned to write an article for which the Government would certainly stop the publication of the paper. Sri Aurobindo had always taken care to give no handle in the editorial articles of the *Bande Mataram* either for a prosecution for sedition or any other drastic action fatal to its existence; an editor of the

Statesman complained that the paper reeked with sedition patently visible between every line, but it was so skilfully written that no legal action could be taken. The manœuvre succeeded and the life of the *Bande Mataram* came to an end in Sri Aurobindo's absence.

The Nationalist programme could only achieve a partial beginning before it was temporarily broken by severe government repression. Its most important practical item was Swadeshi plus Boycott; for Swadeshi much was done to make the idea general and a few beginnings were made, but the greater results showed themselves only afterwards in the course of time. Sri Aurobindo was anxious that this part of the movement should be not only propagated in idea but given a practical organisation and an effective force. He wrote from Baroda asking whether it would not be possible to bring in the industrialists and manufacturers and gain the financial support of landed magnates and create an organisation in which men of industrial and commercial ability and experience and not politicians alone could direct operations and devise means of carrying out the policy; but he was told that it was impossible, the industrialists and the landed magnates were too timid to join in the movement, and the big commercial men were all interested in the import of British goods and therefore on the side of the status quo: so he had to abandon his idea of the organisation of Swadeshi and Boycott. Both Tilak and Sri Aurobindo were in favour of an effective boycott of British goods — but of British goods only; for there was little in the country to replace foreign articles: so they recommended the substitution for the British of foreign goods from Germany and Austria and America so that the fullest pressure might be brought upon England. They wanted the Boycott to be a political weapon and not merely an aid to Swadeshi; the total boycott of all foreign goods was an impracticable idea and the very limited application of it recommended in Congress resolutions was too small to be politically effective. They were for national self-sufficiency in key industries, the production of necessities and of all manufactures of which India had the natural means, but complete self-sufficiency or autarchy did not seem practicable or even desirable since a free India would need to export goods as well as supply them for internal consumption and for that she must import as well and maintain an international exchange. But the sudden enthusiasm for the boycott of all foreign goods was wide and sweeping and the leaders had to conform to this popular cry and be content with the impulse it gave to the Swadeshi idea. National education was another item to which Sri Aurobindo attached much importance. He had been disgusted with the education given by the British system in the schools and colleges and universities, a system of which as a professor in the Baroda College he had full experience. He felt that it tended to dull and impoverish and tie up the naturally quick and brilliant and supple Indian intelligence, to teach it bad intellectual habits and spoil by narrow information and mechanical instruction its originality and productivity. The movement began well and many national schools were established in Bengal and many able men became teachers, but still the development was insufficient and the economical position of the schools precarious. Sri Aurobindo had decided to take up the movement personally and see whether it could not be given a greater expansion and a stronger foundation, but his departure from Bengal cut short this plan. In the repression and the general depression caused by it, most of the schools failed to survive. The idea lived on and it may be hoped that it will one day find an adequate form and body. The idea of people's courts was taken up and worked in some districts, not without success, but this too perished in the storm. The idea of volunteer groupings had a stronger vitality; it lived on, took shape, multiplied its formations and its workers were the spearhead of the movement of direct action which broke out from time to time in the struggle for freedom. The purely political elements of the Nationalist programme and activities were those which lasted and after each wave of repression and depression renewed the thread of the life of the movement for liberation and kept it recognisably one throughout nearly fifty years of its struggle. But the greatest thing done in those years was the creation of a new spirit in the country. In the enthusiasm that swept surging everywhere with the cry of Bande Mataram ringing on all sides men felt it glorious to be alive and dare and act together and hope; the old apathy and timidity was broken and a force created which nothing could destroy and which rose again and again in wave after wave till it carried India to the beginning of a complete victory.

After the *Bande Mataram* case, Sri Aurobindo became the recognised leader of Nationalism in Bengal. He led the party at the session of the Bengal Provincial Conference at Midnapore where there was a vehement clash between the two parties. He now for the first time became a speaker on the public platform, addressed large meetings at Surat and presided over the Nationalist conference there. He stopped at several places on his way back to Calcutta and was the speaker at large meetings called to hear him. He led the party again at the session of the Provincial Conference at Hooghly. There it became evident for the first time that Nationalism was gaining the ascendant, for it commanded a majority among the delegates and in the Subjects Committee Sri Aurobindo was able to defeat the Moderates' resolution welcoming the Reforms and pass his own resolution stigmatising them as utterly inadequate and unreal and rejecting them. But the Moderate leaders threatened to secede if this was maintained and to avoid a scission he consented to allow the Moderate resolution to pass, but spoke at the public session explaining his decision and asking the Nationalists to acquiesce in it in spite of their victory so as to keep some unity in the political forces of Bengal. The Nationalist delegates, at first triumphant and clamorous, accepted the decision and left the hall quietly at Sri Aurobindo's order so that they might not have to vote either for or against the Moderate resolution. This caused much amazement and discomfiture in the minds of the Moderate leaders who complained that the people had refused to listen to their old and tried leaders and clamoured against them, but at the bidding of a young man new to politics they had obeyed in disciplined silence as if a single body.

About this period Sri Aurobindo had decided to take up charge of a Bengali daily, *Nava Shakti*, and had moved from his rented house in Scotts Lane, where he had been living with his wife and sister, to rooms in the office of this newspaper, and there, before he could begin this new venture, early one morning while he was still sleeping, the police charged up the stairs, revolvers in hand, and arrested him. He was taken to the police station and thence to Alipur Jail where he remained for a year during the magistrate's investigation and the trial in the Sessions Court at Alipur. At first he was lodged for some time in a solitary cell but afterwards transferred to a large section of the jail where he lived in one huge room with the other prisoners in the case; subsequently, after the assassination of the approver in the jail, all the prisoners were confined in contiguous but separate cells and met only in the court or in the daily exercise where they could not speak to each other. It was in the second period that Sri Aurobindo made the acquaintance of most of his fellow accused. In the jail he spent almost all his time in reading the Gita and the Upanishads and in intensive meditation and the practice of Yoga. This he pursued even in the second interval when he had no opportunity of being alone and had to accustom himself to meditation amid general talk and laughter, the playing of games and much noise and disturbance; in the first and third periods he had full opportunity and used it to the full. In the Sessions Court the accused were confined in a large prisoner's cage and here during the whole day he remained absorbed in his meditation, attending little to the trial and hardly listening to the evidence. C. R. Das, one of his Nationalist collaborators and a famous lawyer, had put aside his large practice and devoted himself for months to the defence of Sri Aurobindo, who left the case entirely to him and troubled no more about it; for he had been assured from within and knew that he would be acquitted. During this period his view of life was radically changed; he had taken up Yoga with the original idea of acquiring spiritual force and energy and divine guidance for his work in life. But now the inner spiritual life and realisation which had continually been increasing in magnitude and universality and assuming a larger place took him up entirely and his work became a part and result of it and besides far exceeded the service and liberation of the country and fixed itself in an aim, previously only glimpsed, which was world-wide in its bearing and concerned with the whole future of humanity.

When he came out from jail Sri Aurobindo found the whole political aspect of the country altered; most of the Nationalist leaders were in jail or in self-imposed exile and there was a general discouragement and depression, though the feeling in the country had not ceased but was only suppressed and was growing by its suppression. He determined to continue the struggle; he held weekly meetings in Calcutta, but the attendance which had numbered formerly thousands full of enthusiasm, was now only of hundreds and had no longer the same force and life. He also went to places in the districts to speak and at one of these delivered his speech at Uttarpara in which for the first time he spoke publicly of his Yoga and his spiritual experiences. He started also two weeklies, one in English and one in

Bengali, the *Karmayogin* and *Dharma* which had a fairly large circulation and were, unlike the *Bande Mataram*, easily self-supporting. He attended and spoke at the Provincial Conference at Barisal in 1909: for in Bengal owing to the compromise at Hooghly the two parties had not split altogether apart and both joined in the Conference though there could be no representatives of the Nationalist party at the meeting of the Central Moderate Body which had taken the place of the Congress. Surendra Nath Banerji had indeed called a private conference attended by Sri Aurobindo and one or two other leaders of the Nationalists to discuss a project of uniting the two parties at the session in Benares and giving a joint fight to the dominant right wing of the Moderates; for he had always dreamt of becoming again leader of a united Bengal with the Extremist party as his strong right-arm: but that would have necessitated the Nationalists being appointed as delegates by the Bengal Moderates and accepting the constitution imposed at Surat. This Sri Aurobindo refused to do; he demanded a change in that constitution enabling newly formed associations to elect delegates so that the Nationalists might independently send their representatives to the All-India session and on this point the negotiations broke down. Sri Aurobindo began however to consider how to revive the national movement under the changed circumstances. He glanced at the possibility of falling back on a Home Rule movement which the Government could not repress, but this, which was actually realised by Mrs. Besant later on, would have meant a postponement and a falling back from the ideal of independence. He looked also at the possibility of an intense and organised passive resistance movement in the manner afterwards adopted by Gandhi. He saw, however, that he himself could not be the leader of such a movement.

At no time did he consent to have anything to do with the sham Reforms which were all the Government at that period cared to offer. He held up always the slogan of "no compromise" or, as he now put it in his Open Letter to his countrymen published in the *Karmayogin*, "no cooperation without control". It was only if real political, administrative and financial control were given to popular ministers in an elected Assembly that he would have anything to do with offers from the British Government. Of this he saw no sign until the proposal of the Montagu Reforms in which first something of the kind seemed to appear. He foresaw that the British Government would have to begin trying to meet the national aspiration half-way, but he would not anticipate that moment before it actually came. The Montagu Reforms came nine years after Sri Aurobindo had retired to Pondicherry and by that time he had abandoned all outward and public political activity in order to devote himself to his spiritual work, acting only by his spiritual force on the movement in India, until his prevision of real negotiations between the British Government and the Indian leaders was fulfilled by the Cripps' proposal and the events that came after.

Meanwhile the Government were determined to get rid of Sri Aurobindo as the only considerable obstacle left to the success of their repressive policy. As they could not send him to the Andamans they decided to deport him. This came to the knowledge of Sister Nivedita and she informed Sri Aurobindo and asked him to leave British India and work from outside so that his work would not be stopped or totally interrupted. Sri Aurobindo contented himself with publishing in the *Karmayogin* a signed article in which he spoke of the project of deportation and left the country what he called his last will and testament; he felt sure that this would kill the idea of deportation and in fact it so turned out. Deportation left aside the Government could only wait for some opportunity for prosecution for sedition and this chance came to them when Sri Aurobindo published in the same paper another signed article reviewing the political situation. The article was sufficiently moderate in its tone and later on the High Court refused to regard it as seditious and acquitted the printer. Sri Aurobindo one night at the *Karmayogin* office received information of the Government's intention to search the office and arrest him. While considering what should be his attitude, he received a sudden command from above to go to Chandernagore in French India. He obeyed the command at once, for it was now his rule to move only as he was moved by the divine guidance and never to resist and depart from it; he did not stay to consult with anyone, but in ten minutes was at the river ghat and in a boat plying on the Ganges, in a few hours he was at Chandernagore where he went into secret residence. He sent a message to Sister Nivedita asking her to take up the editing of the *Karmayogin* in his absence. This was the end of his active connection with his two journals. At Chandernagore he plunged entirely into solitary meditation and ceased all other activity. Then there came to him a call to proceed to Pondicherry. A boat manned by some young revolutionaries of Uttarpara took him to Calcutta; there he boarded the *Dupleix* and reached Pondicherry on 4 April 1910.

At Pondicherry, from this time onwards Sri Aurobindo's practice of Yoga became more and more absorbing. He dropped all participation in any public political activity, refused more than one request to preside at sessions of the restored Indian National Congress and made a rule of abstention from any public utterance of any kind not connected with his spiritual activities or any contribution of writings or articles except what he wrote afterwards in the *Arya*. For some years he kept up some private communication with the revolutionary forces he had led through one or two individuals, but this also he dropped after a time and his abstention from any kind of participation in politics became complete. As his vision of the future grew clearer, he saw that the eventual independence of India was assured by the march of Forces of which he became aware, that Britain would be compelled by the pressure of Indian resistance and by the pressure of international events to concede independence and that she was already moving towards that eventuality with whatever opposition and reluctance. He felt that there would be no need of armed insurrection and that the secret preparation for it could be dropped without injury to the nationalist cause, although the revolutionary spirit had to be maintained and would be maintained intact. His own personal intervention in politics would therefore be no longer indispensable. Apart from all this, the magnitude of the spiritual work set before him became more and more clear to him, and he saw that the concentration of all his energies on it was necessary. Accordingly, when the Ashram came into existence, he kept it free from all political connections or action; even when he intervened in politics twice afterwards on special occasions, this intervention was purely personal and the Ashram was not concerned in it. The British Government and numbers of people besides could not believe that Sri Aurobindo had ceased from all political action and it was supposed by them that he was secretly participating in revolutionary activities and even creating a secret organisation in the security of French India. But all this was pure imagination and rumour and there

Sri Aurobindo

The Mother

Sri Aurobindo writing the "Arya"

The Ashram Main Entrance

The Samadhi of Sri Aurobindo and the Mother

The Ashram Printing Press

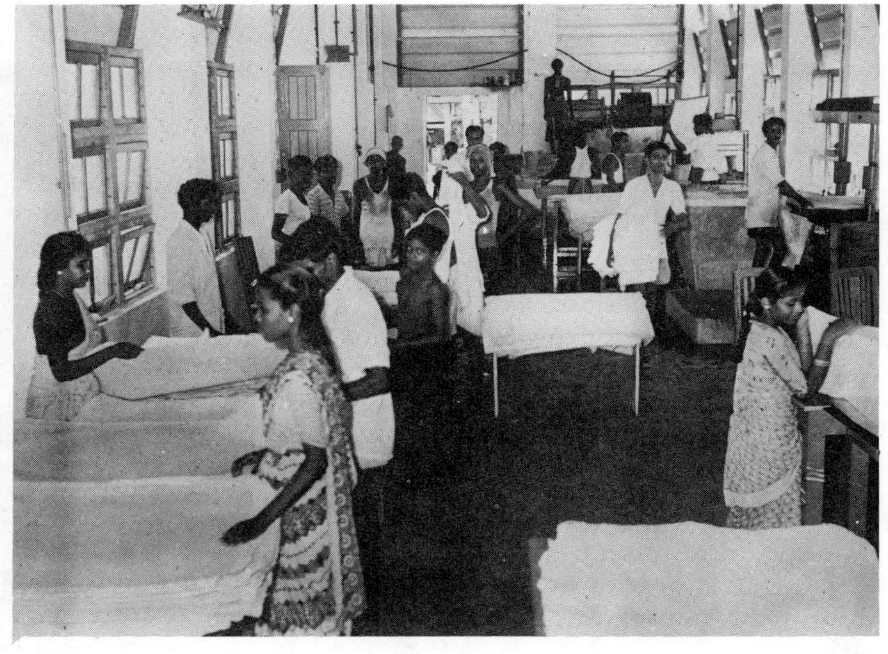

The Hand Made Paper Factory

The Harpagon Workshop

The Dining Hall

The Dining Hall

The International Centre of Education

The Courtyard of the Centre of Education

The Technical Lab of the Centre of Education

The March Past in the Playground

In the Sportsground

The Mother

was nothing of the kind. His retirement from political activity was complete, just as was his personal retirement into solitude in 1910.

But this did not mean, as most people supposed, that he had retired into some height of spiritual experience devoid of any further interest in the world or in the fate of India. It could not mean that, for the very principle of his Yoga was not only to realise the Divine and attain to a complete spiritual consciousness, but also to take all life and all world activity into the scope of this spiritual consciousness and action and to base life on the Spirit and give it a spiritual meaning. In his retirement Sri Aurobindo kept a close watch on all that was happening in the world and in India and actively intervened whenever necessary, but solely with a spiritual force and silent spiritual action; for it is part of the experience of those who have advanced far in yoga that besides the ordinary forces and activities of the mind and life and body in Matter, there are other forces and powers that can act and do act from behind and from above; there is also a spiritual dynamic power which can be possessed by those who are advanced in the spiritual consciousness, though all do not care to possess or, possessing, to use it and this power is greater than any other and more effective. It was this force which, as soon as he attained to it, he used, at first only in a limited field of personal work, but afterwards in a constant action upon the world forces. He had no reason to be dissatisfied with the results or to feel the necessity of any other kind of action. Twice however he found it advisable to take in addition other action of a public kind. The first was in relation to the second World War. At the beginning he did not actively concern himself with it, but when it appeared as if Hitler would crush all the forces opposed to him and Nazism dominate the world, he began to intervene. He declared himself publicly on the side of the Allies, made some financial contributions in answer to the appeal for funds and encouraged those who sought his advice to enter the army or share in the war effort. Inwardly, he put his spiritual force behind the Allies from the moment of Dunkirk when everybody was expecting the immediate fall of England and the definite triumph of Hitler, and he had the satisfaction of seeing the rush of German victory almost immediately arrested and the tide of war begin to turn in the opposite direction. This he did, because he saw that behind Hitler and Nazism were dark Asuric forces and that their success would mean the enslavement of mankind to the tyranny of evil, and a set-back to the course of evolution and especially to the spiritual evolution of mankind: it would lead also to the enslavement not only of Europe but of Asia, and in it India, an enslavement far more terrible than any this country had ever endured, and the undoing of all the work that had been done for her liberation. It was this reason also that induced him to support publicly the Cripps' offer and to press the Congress leaders to accept it. He had not, for various reasons, intervened with his spiritual force against the Japanese aggression until it became evident that Japan intended to attack and even invade and conquer India. He allowed certain letters he had written in support of the war affirming his views of the Asuric nature and inevitable outcome of Hitlerism to become public. He supported the Cripps' offer because by its acceptance India and Britain could stand united against the Asuric forces and the solution of Cripps' could be used as a step towards independence. When negotiations failed, Sri Aurobindo returned to his reliance on the use of spiritual force alone against the aggressor and had the satisfaction of seeing the tide of Japanese victory, which had till then swept everything before it, change immediately into a tide of rapid, crushing and finally immense and overwhelming defeat. He had also after a time the satisfaction of seeing his previsions about the future of India justify themselves so that she stands independent with whatever internal difficulties.

III

THE FIFTEENTH OF AUGUST 1947

(A Message written by Sri Aurobindo for
broadcast over All India Radio)

August 15th is the birthday of free India. It marks for her the end of
an old era, the beginning of a new age. But it has a significance not
only for us, but for Asia and the whole world; for it signifies the entry
into the comity of nations of a new power with untold potentialities
which has a great part to play in determining the political, social,
cultural and spiritual future of humanity. To me personally it must
naturally be gratifying that this date which was notable only for me
because it was my own birthday celebrated annually by those who
have accepted my gospel of life, should have acquired this vast
significance. As a mystic, I take this identification, not as a coinci-
dence or fortuitous accident, but as a sanction and seal of the Divine
Power which guides my steps on the work with which I began life.
Indeed almost all the world movements which I hoped to see fulfilled
in my lifetime, though at that time they looked like impossible
dreams, I can observe on this day either approaching fruition or
initiated and on the way to their achievement.

I have been asked for a message on this great occasion, but I am
perhaps hardly in a position to give one. All I can do is to make a
personal declaration of the aims and ideals conceived in my childhood and youth and now watched in their beginning of fulfilment,
because they are relevant to the freedom of India, since they are a
part of what I believe to be India's future work, something in which
she cannot but take a leading position. For I have always held and
said that India was arising, not to serve her own material interests
only, to achieve expansion, greatness, power and prosperity, –
though these too she must not neglect –, and certainly not like others
to acquire domination of other peoples, but to live also for God and
the world as a helper and leader of the whole human race. Those
aims and ideals were in their natural order these: a revolution which
would achieve India's freedom and her unity; the resurgence and

liberation of Asia and her return to the great role which she had played in the progress of human civilisation; the rise of a new, a greater, brighter and nobler life for mankind which for its entire realisation would rest outwardly on an international unification of the separate existence of the peoples, preserving and securing their national life but drawing them together into an overriding and consummating oneness; the gift by India of her spiritual knowledge and her means for the spiritualisation of life to the whole race; finally, a new step in the evolution which, by uplifting the consciousness to a higher level, would begin the solution of the many problems of existence which have perplexed and vexed humanity, since men began to think and to dream of individual perfection and a perfect society.

India is free but she has not achieved unity, only a fissured and broken freedom. At one time it almost seemed as if she might relapse into the chaos of separate States which preceded the British conquest. Fortunately there has now developed a strong possibility that this disastrous relapse will be avoided. The wisely drastic policy of the Constituent Assembly makes it possible that the problem of the depressed classes will be solved without schism or fissure. But the old communal division into Hindu and Muslim seems to have hardened into the figure of a permanent political division of the country. It is to be hoped that the Congress and the nation will not accept the settled fact as for ever settled or as anything more than a temporary expedient. For if it lasts, India may be seriously weakened, even crippled: civil strife may remain always possible, possible even a new invasion and foreign conquest. The partition of the country must go, – it is to be hoped by a slackening of tension, by a progressive understanding of the need of peace and concord, by the constant necessity of common and concerted action, even of an instrument of union for that purpose. In this way unity may come about under whatever form – the exact form may have a pragmatic but not a fundamental importance. But by whatever means, the division must and will go. For without it the destiny of India might be seriously impaired and even frustrated. But that must not be.

Asia has arisen and large parts of it have been liberated or are at this moment being liberated; its other still subject parts are moving through whatever struggles towards freedom. Only a little has to be done and that will be done today or tomorrow. There India has her part to play and has begun to play it with an energy and ability which already indicate the measure of her possibilities and the place she can take in the council of the nations.

The unification of mankind is under way, though only in an imperfect initiative, organised but struggling against tremendous difficulties. But the momentum is there and, if the experience of history can be taken as a guide, it must inevitably increase until it conquers. Here too India has begun to play a prominent part and, if she can develop that larger statesmanship which is not limited by the present facts and immediate possibilities but looks into the future and brings it nearer, her presence may make all the difference between a slow and timid and a bold and swift development. A catastrophe may intervene and interrupt or destroy what is being done, but even then the final result is sure. For in any case the unification is a necessity in the course of Nature, an inevitable movement and its achievement can be safely foretold. Its necessity for the nations also is clear, for without it the freedom of the small peoples can never be safe hereafter and even large and powerful nations cannot really be secure. India, if she remains divided, will not herself be sure of her safety. It is therefore to the interest of all that union should take place. Only human imbecility and stupid selfishness could prevent it. Against that, it has been said, even the gods strive in vain; but it cannot stand for ever against the necessity of Nature and the Divine Will. Nationalism will then have fulfilled itself; an international spirit and outlook must grow up and international forms and institutions; even it may be such developments as dual or multilateral citizenship and a voluntary fusion of cultures may appear in the process of the change and the spirit of nationalism losing its militancy may find these things perfectly compatible with the integrity of its own outlook. A new spirit of oneness will take hold of the human race.

The spiritual gift of India to the world has already begun. India's spirituality is entering Europe and America in an ever increasing measure. That movement will grow; amid the disasters of the time more and more eyes are turning towards her with hope and there is even an increasing resort not only to her teachings, but to her psychic and spiritual practice.

The rest is still a personal hope and an idea and ideal which has begun to take hold both in India and in the West on forward-looking minds. The difficulties in the way are more formidable than in any other field of endeavour, but difficulties were made to be overcome and if the Supreme Will is there, they will be overcome. Here too, if this evolution is to take place, since it must come through a growth of the spirit and the inner consciousness, the initiative can come from India and although the scope must be universal, the central movement may be hers.

Such is the content which I put into this date of India's liberation; whether or how far or how soon this connection will be fulfilled, depends upon this new and free India.

IV

SPIRITUAL LIFE

(Compiled from notes and letters of Sri Aurobindo)

Sri Aurobindo began his practice of yoga in 1904. Even before this, several experiences had come to him spontaneously, "of themselves and with a sudden unexpectedness". There was, for instance, the mental experience of the *atman* or true Self, which he had while reading the Upanishads in London in 1892. The next year a "vast calm" descended upon him the moment he stepped on Indian soil after his long absence in England. This calm surrounded him and remained for many months afterwards. Also in 1893 Sri Aurobindo had a vision of the Godhead surging up from within when he was in danger of a carriage accident. In 1903, while walking on the ridge of the Takht-i-Suleman in Kashmir, he had the "realisation of the vacant Infinite", and a year or two later he experienced the "living presence of Kali" in a shrine on the banks of the Narmada.

In 1904 Sri Aurobindo began yoga with the "assiduous practice of *pranayama*". Around this time he met the yogi Brahmananda and was "greatly impressed by him", but he had no helper or guru in yoga until January 1908, when he met the Maharashtrian yogi Vishnu Bhaskar Lele. Lele showed Sri Aurobindo how to establish complete silence of mind and immobility of consciousness. Within three days Sri Aurobindo succeeded in achieving this state that sometimes requires a lifetime of yoga to attain. The result was a series of "lasting and massive spiritual realisations which opened to him the larger ways of yoga". Lele finally told Sri Aurobindo to put himself entirely into the hands of the Divine within and to move only as he was moved by Him. This henceforward became the whole foundation and principle of Sri Aurobindo's sadhana. Sri Aurobindo and Lele parted ways after a month or two, and from this time until the Mother came to India Sri Aurobindo received no spiritual help from anyone.

In 1908 and 1909, while Sri Aurobindo was an undertrial prisoner in the Alipur Jail, he had the constant vision of the omnipresent

Godhead: "I looked at the jail that secluded me from men and it was no longer by its high walls that I was imprisoned; no, it was Vasudeva who surrounded me. I walked under the branches of the tree in front of my cell, but it was not a tree, I knew it was Vasudeva, it was Sri Krishna whom I saw standing there and holding over me his shade. I looked at the bars of my cell, the very grating that did duty for a door and again I saw Vasudeva. It was Narayana who was guarding and standing sentry over me. Or I lay on the coarse blankets that were given me for a couch and felt the arms of Sri Krishna around me, the arms of my Friend and Lover.... I looked at the prisoners in the jail, the thieves, the murderers, the swindlers, and as I looked at them I saw Vasudeva, it was Narayana whom I found in these darkened souls and misused bodies."

In the jail Sri Aurobindo spent much of his time reading the Gita and Upanishads, meditating and practising yoga. Even in the court-room he remained absorbed in meditation, attending little to the trial and hardly listening to the evidence. During this period his view of life was radically changed; he had originally taken up yoga with the idea of acquiring spiritual force and energy and divine guidance for his political work. But now his inner spiritual life and realisation, which was continually increasing in magnitude and universality, assumed a larger place and took him up entirely. His work became a part and result of it, far exceeding in its scope the service and liberation of the country; it fixed itself in an aim, previously only glimpsed, which was world-wide in its bearing and concerned with the whole future of humanity.

Sri Aurobindo's yoga and spiritual philosophy are founded on four great realisations. Two of these he had realised in full before his coming to Pondicherry in 1910. The first, the realisation of the silent, spaceless and timeless Brahman, he had gained while meditating with Lele in 1908. The feeling and perception of the total unreality of the world which at first attended this realisation disappeared after the second realisation, which was gained in the Alipur Jail in 1908 or 1909 – the realisation of the cosmic consciousness and the vision of the Divine as all beings and as all that is. In his meditations in the jail Sri Aurobindo was already on his way to the other two realisations – that of the supreme Reality with the static and dynamic Brahman as its two aspects and that of the higher planes of consciousness leading to the Supermind.

By 1912 the third realisation was attained when Sri Aurobindo experienced an "abiding realisation and dwelling in Parabrahman" (the supreme Reality). The process of ascent into the higher planes of consciousness and of bringing down the power of those planes into the physical consciousness continued. On 24 November 1926 this effort was crowned by the descent of the "Godhead of the Overmind", the highest of the planes between Mind and Supermind, into the physical. This descent was preparatory to the descent of the Supermind itself, by which "the perfection dreamed of by all that is highest in humanity can come". From 1926 Sri Aurobindo worked spiritually to bring about the supramental descent, and in 1950 left his physical body to hasten its advent.

V

THE TEACHING OF SRI AUROBINDO

The teaching of Sri Aurobindo.starts from that of the ancient sages of India that behind the appearances of the universe there is the Reality of a Being and Consciousness, a Self of all things, one and eternal. All beings are united in that One Self and Spirit but divided by a certain separativity of consciousness, an ignorance of their true Self and Reality in the mind, life and body. It is possible by a certain psychological discipline to remove this veil of seperative consciousness and become aware of the true Self, the Divinity within us and all.

Sri Aurobindo's teaching states that this One Being and Consciousness is involved here in Matter. Evolution is the process by which it liberates itself; consciousness appears in what seems to be inconscient and once having appeared is self-impelled to grow higher and at the same time to enlarge and develop towards a greater and greater perfection. Life is the first step of this release of consciousness; mind is the second; but the evolution does not finish with mind, it awaits a release into something greater, a consciousness which is spiritual and supramental. The next step of the evolution must be towards the development of Supermind and Spirit as the dominant power in the conscious being. For only then will the involved Divinity in things release itself entirely and it become possible for life to manifest perfection.

But while the former steps in evolution were taken by Nature without a conscious will in the plant and animal life, in man Nature becomes able to evolve by a conscious will in the instrument. It is not, however, by the mental will in man that this can be wholly done, for the mind goes only to a certain point and after that can only move in a circle. A conversion has to be made, a turning of the consciousness by which mind has to change into the higher principle. This method is to be found through the ancient psychological discipline and practice of Yoga. In the past, it has been attempted by a drawing away from the world and a disappearance into the height of the Self or Spirit. Sri Aurobindo teaches that a descent of the higher principle is possible which will not merely release the spiritual Self out of the world, but release it in the world, replace the mind's ignorance or its very limited knowledge by a supramental Truth-Consciousness which will be a sufficient instrument of the inner Self and make it possible for the human being to find himself dynamically as well as inwardly and grow out of his still animal humanity into a diviner race. The psychological discipline of Yoga can be used to that end by opening all the parts of the being to a conversion or transformation through the descent and working of the higher still concealed supramental principle.

This, however, cannot be done at once or in a short time or by any rapid or miraculous transformation. Many steps have to be taken by the seeker before the supramental descent is possible. Man lives mostly in his surface mind, life and body, but there is an inner being within him with greater possibilities to which he has to awake – for it is only a very restricted influence from it that he receives now and that pushes him to a constant pursuit of a greater beauty, harmony, power and knowledge. The first process of Yoga is therefore to open the ranges of this inner being and to live from there outward, governing his outward life by an inner light and force. In doing so he discovers in himself his true soul which is not this outer mixture of mental, vital and physical elements but something of the Reality behind them, a spark from the one Divine Fire. He has to learn to live in his soul and purify and orientate by its drive towards the Truth the rest of the nature. There can follow afterwards an opening upward and descent of a higher principle of the Being. But even then it is not at once the full supramental Light and Force. For there are several ranges of consciousness between the ordinary human mind and the supramental Truth-Consciousness. These intervening ranges have to be opened up and their power brought down into the mind, life and body. Only afterwards can the full power of the Truth-Consciousness work in the nature. The process of this self-discipline or sadhana is therefore long and difficult, but even a little of it is so much gained because it makes the ultimate release and perfection more possible.

There are many things belonging to older systems that are necessary on the way – an opening of the mind to a greater wideness and to the sense of the Self and the Infinite, an emergence into what has been called the cosmic consciousness, mastery over the desires and passions; an outward asceticism is not essential, but the conquest of desire and attachment and a control over the body and its needs, greeds and instincts are indispensable. There is a combination of the principles of the old systems, the way of knowledge through the mind's discernment between Reality and the appearance, the heart's way of devotion, love and surrender and the way of works turning the will away from motives of self-interest to the Truth and the service of a greater Reality than the ego. For the whole being has to be trained so that it can respond and be transformed when it is possible for that greater Light and Force to work in the nature.

In this discipline the inspiration of the Master and, in the difficult stages, his control and his presence are indispensable – for it would be impossible otherwise to go through it without much stumbling and error which would prevent all chance of success. The Master is one who has risen to a higher consciousness and being and he is often regarded as its manifestation or representative. He not only helps by his teaching and still more by his influence and example but by a power to communicate his own experience to others.

This is Sri Aurobindo's teaching and method of practice. It is not his object to develop any one religion or to amalgamate the older religions or to found any new religion – for any of these things would lead away from his central purpose. The one aim of his Yoga is an inner self-development by which each one who follows it can in time discover the One Self in all and evolve a higher consciousness than the mental, a spiritual and supramental consciousness which will transform and divinise human nature.

VI

A SKETCH OF THE MOTHER'S LIFE

The Mother was born in Paris on 21 February 1878. Mirra, as the child was named, was the daughter of the banker Maurice Alfassa (born in Adrianople, Turkey, in 1843), and Mathilde Ismaloun (born in Alexandria, Egypt, in 1857). Maurice, his wife, and their son Mattéo (born in Alexandria in 1876) emigrated from Egypt to France a year before Mirra's birth. Her early education was given at home. Around 1892 she went to a studio to learn drawing and painting, and later studied art at the famous École des Beaux Arts. Besides being an accomplished painter (some of her works were exhibited at the Paris Salon), the Mother was a talented musician and writer.

Concerning her early spiritual life, the Mother has said: "Between 11 and 13 a series of psychic and spiritual experiences revealed to me not only the existence of God but man's possibility of uniting with Him, of realising Him integrally in consciousness and action, of manifesting Him upon earth in a life divine." Around 1905 the Mother journeyed to Tlemcen, Algeria, where she studied occultism for two years with a Polish or Russian adept, Max Théon, and his wife. Returning to Paris in 1906, she started her first group of spiritual seekers. Between 1911 and 1913 she gave many talks to various groups in Paris.

At the age of thirty-six the Mother came to Pondicherry. Here, on 29 March 1914, she met Sri Aurobindo. At once she recognised him as the master who for many years had inwardly been guiding her spiritual development. After staying in India for eleven months, she was obliged to return to France because of the first world war. She left France after about a year, and lived for almost four years in Japan. On 24 April 1920 the Mother returned to Pondicherry and resumed her collaboration with Sri Aurobindo. She remained in India for the rest of her life.

At the time the Mother rejoined Sri Aurobindo, a small group of disciples had gathered around him. After her coming the number of disciples increased. Eventually this informal grouping took shape as an ashram or spiritual community.

From its very beginning in November 1926, Sri Aurobindo entrusted the full material and spiritual charge of the Sri Aurobindo Ashram to the Mother. Under her guidance, which extended over nearly fifty years, the Ashram has grown into a many-faceted community which at present consists of about 1200 persons. Among the Mother's other achievements during this period were the creation of the Sri Aurobindo International Centre of Education and the initiation of Auroville. On 17 November 1973, at the age of ninety-five the Mother left her body.

VII

SRI AUROBINDO ASHRAM

This Ashram has been created with another object than that ordinarily common to such institutions, not for the renunciation of the world but as a centre and a field of practice for the evolution of another kind and form of life which would in the final end be moved by a higher spiritual consciousness and embody a greater life of the spirit.

Sri Aurobindo

DEVELOPMENT

For years after his arrival in Pondicherry in 1910, Sri Aurobindo was unwilling to speak of his household as an Ashram. Not that the term would have been inappropriate, for an Ashram is simply "the house or houses of a Teacher or Master of spiritual philosophy in which he receives and lodges those who come to him for the teaching and practice."* It is true that in the early days Sri Aurobindo took no disciples as such. He once wrote, "With the three or four young men who accompanied me or joined me in Pondicherry, I had at first the relation of friends and companions rather than of a Guru and disciples; it was on the ground of politics I had come to know them and not on the spiritual ground. Afterwards only there was a gradual development of spiritual relations." But even as more and more aspirants gathered around Sri Aurobindo specifically to practise yoga under his direction, the grouping remained informal, and was not referred to as an "ashram".

It was only after the Mother finally settled in Pondicherry in 1920 that an attempt was made at collective organisation. "The number of disciples then showed a tendency to increase rather rapidly." And as thus "the Ashram began to develop, it fell to the Mother to organise it." She had to see to the outward lives of the disciples, whose "numbers began so much to increase that it was thought necessary to make an arrangement for lodging those who came, and houses were bought and rented according to need for the purpose. Arrange-

* This and the following quotations are taken from various works of Sri Aurobindo and the Mother.

ments [also] had to be made for the maintenance, repair, rebuilding of houses, for the service of food and for decent living and hygiene" and so forth. At the same time the guidance of the disciples' inner lives began progressively to pass into the Mother's hands, so that, when Sri Aurobindo retired into seclusion on 24 November 1926, "the whole material and spiritual charge" of what had now come to be called Sri Aurobindo's ashram "devolved on her". It was in this way that "the Ashram was founded or rather founded itself in 1926", the informal grouping of seekers taking "the form of an ashram more from the wish of the sadhaks who desired to entrust their whole inner and outer life to the Mother than from any intention or plan of hers or of Sri Aurobindo's".

The Sri Aurobindo Ashram is thus more a spontaneous growth than a deliberate creation. But it is also the realisation of an intention that had long been cherished by the Mother. She once remarked:

"At the beginning of my present earthly existence I was put into touch with many people who said they had a great inner aspiration, an urge towards something deeper and truer, but were tied down, subjected, slaves of that brutal necessity of earning their living, and that this weighed down upon them so much, took away so much of their time and energy that they could not engage in any other activity, inner or outer. I heard that very often.

"I was very young at that time, and always I used to tell myself that if ever I could do it, I would try to create a little world – Oh! quite a small one, but still – a small world where people would be able to live without having to be preoccupied by problems of food and lodging and clothing and the imperious necessities of life, to see if all the energies freed by this certainty of an assured material living would spontaneously be turned towards the divine life and inner realisation."

The conditions of basic material security that the Ashram, as it took shape, provided to an ever increasing number of disciples, permitted their spiritual lives to unfold in the light of Sri Aurobindo and under the Mother's constant daily care.

In the half-century since its founding the Sri Aurobindo Ashram has grown from an informal grouping of two dozen sadhaks into a diversified spiritual community with 1200 members. There is, besides, a significant number of non-members living in Pondicherry who take part in the Ashram's life. All regions of India, and many countries of Asia, Europe and America are represented. Members are of both sexes and of all ages. No distinctions of creed, caste or national origin are observed.

Once confined to a few buildings in one corner of Pondicherry, the Ashram's growth has caused it to expand physically in all directions. Today Ashramites live and work in more than 400 buildings spread throughout the town. The central focus of the community is one group of houses including those in which Sri Aurobindo and the Mother dwelt for most of their lives in Pondicherry. This interconnected block of houses – called "the Ashram main-building", or more usually just "the Ashram" – surrounds a tree-shaded court-yard, at the centre of which lies the flower-covered "Samadhi". This white marble shrine holds, in two separate chambers, the mortal remains of Sri Aurobindo and the Mother.

CHARACTER

In the popular imagination ashrams are connected with hermitages or religious orders, but in fact "an ashram is not an association or a religious body or a monastery". The Sri Aurobindo Ashram in particular has nothing to do with asceticism or retreat from the world. The character of this unique institution stems from the special nature of Sri Aurobindo's teaching. This may be summed up in these words from one of his letters:

"The way of Yoga followed here has a purpose different from others, – for its aim is not only to rise out of the ordinary ignorant world-consciousness into the divine consciousness, but to bring the supramental power of that divine consciousness down into the ignorance of mind, life and body, to transform them, to manifest the Divine here and create a divine life in Matter."

As this aim of Sri Aurobindo's yoga differs from that of traditional yogic systems, so the ashram that grew up around him "is not an. ashram like others". As in all spiritual communities, life in the Sri Aurobindo Ashram is centred around the practice of a discipline for the attainment of the goal common to all yogas and religions – Spirit,

Self, God, divinity, perfection. But in the Ashram the discipline does not follow any fixed method, but is "an inner practice conducted under the spiritual guidance and influence of Sri Aurobindo and the Mother". The guidance, given by them in innumerable talks and letters, is now available in numerous books. The influence is something that can be felt inwardly by all who have an opening. This self-opening is one of the three main leverages of the yoga, the others being a progressive surrender to the spiritual force within and a rejection of all that opposes its workings. Itself chiefly an inward movement, the rejection assumes outward formulation in three rules – no smoking, drinking or drug-taking, no sex, and no politics. These prohibitions, the only regulations the Ashram imposes on its members, are meant to exclude activities contrary to the right practice of yoga by persons who have consecrated their lives to it.

The way of yoga practised at the Ashram is "a living thing, not a mental principle or a set method to be stuck to against all necessary variations". Sri Aurobindo has amplified on this in his letters: "The general principle of self-consecration and self-giving is the same for all in this yoga, but each has his own way of consecration and self-giving." For "the technique of a world-changing yoga has to be as multiform, sinuous, patient, all-including as the world itself." It is because of this that "the sadhana of this yoga does not proceed through any set mental teaching or prescribed forms of meditation, mantras or others."

Meditation is of course a powerful tool; through it one learns to quieten the mind and open to the higher influence, and also to contact the divine presence in the heart. Some form of meditation or concentration is used by most Ashram members in their individual practice. Collective meditations also are held regularly; these are open to all – visitors as well as Ashramites – who wish to attend. But "meditation can deal only with the inner being"; and since Sri Aurobindo's yoga includes as part of its aim the transformation of the outer consciousness, "meditation alone is not enough". Devotion to a form or embodiment of the Divine is another important aid, but this too is not in itself sufficient. For Sri Aurobindo's is an "integral yoga, that is, a turning of all the being in all its parts to the Divine.... It is not only the heart that has to turn to the Divine and change, but the mind also, so knowledge is necessary, and the will and power of action and creation also, so works too are necessary." Likewise essential for the complete change of the instrumental nature – mind, life and body – is "a seeking for perfection, so that the nature too may become one with the nature of the divine". The integral yoga practised in the Ashram includes all these approaches. It is thus a synthesis of the methods of the four principal paths of traditional yoga – the path of knowledge, the path of devotion, the path of works, and the path of perfection.

In ashrams where liberation from worldly existence (*moksha*) is the sole object, there is a tendency for members to withdraw from outward life – to become *sannyasis* or ascetics. But in accordance with the comprehensive goal of Sri Aurobindo's teaching, members of his Ashram "are not *sannyasis*; [for] it is not *moksha* that is the sole aim of the yoga here". Liberation isof course necessary; but it is an inner freedom and equanimity and not an outward renunciation that is required. From the inner poise, outward activities can and indeed must be carried out; for, as Sri Aurobindo once explained, "What is being done here is a work – a work which will be founded on yogic consciousness and Yoga-Shakti [the divine power], and can have no other foundation. Meanwhile every member here is expected to do some work in the Ashram as a part of this spiritual preparation."

WORK

A community the size of the Sri Aurobindo Ashram naturally requires a considerable amount of work to keep it going. Most of this is done by members. The primary purpose of the work, however, is not to satisfy any practical or economic need, or to be a means for the self-expression of the members, but to provide a field for their spiritual growth. As Sri Aurobindo once wrote, "work done in the Ashram" is done not "as a service to humanity" or even as a service to the sadhaks of the Ashram, but "as a service to the Divine and as a field for the inner opening to the Divine, surrender to the Divine alone, rejection of ego and all the ordinary vital movements and the training in a psychic elevation, selflessness, obedience, renunciation of all mental, vital or other self-assertion of the limited personality". The Mother expressed the same idea more succinctly: "To work for the Divine is to pray with the body."

Work is done by all, and it is done without remuneration. Workers strive for perfection not in hopes of advancement, but in order to make their labour a more fitting offering to the Divine. What is important is not the nature of the work or the amount accomplished, but the attitude in which it is done. In the Ashram work is not graded according to common notions of "high" and "low". In the Mother's words, "It is not what you do that matters, but the way you do it and the consciousness you put into it. Remember the Divine unceasingly, and all that you do will express the Divine Presence. When you consecrate all your actions to the Divine, there will no longer be any higher or lower activities, all will have an equal importance: that conferred on them by the consecration."

During the Mother's lifetime all work was done under her supervision, either directly or through the intermediary of departmental heads. Today the departmental heads remain, but their work is coordinated by a central administration. This arrangement necessarily involves an organisational hierarchy, but this does not imply that sadhaks are considered as superior or inferior according to the type of work that they do. Everyone is seen as part of a diverse but interrelated whole. None is independent, neither the heads of departments nor the workers. The need for cooperation is recognised by all.

Each of the Ashram's departments grew up in answer to a particular need of the community. Essential services, those connected with boarding, lodging, clothing, and health were the first to be organised. Later departments expressive of the Ashram's diverse artistic and cultural life took shape. "We do not want to exclude any of the world's activities", Sri Aurobindo once wrote, and he listed, along with "poetry, art and literature", such fields as trade and industry as forming necessary parts of a total spiritual community. As the Ashram began to expand into these and other areas, some disciples were entrusted with responsibility over administration and accounts. Information about the workings of the departments in each of these categories is given below.

The Sri Aurobindo Ashram provides its members with everything they need for a decent and healthy life. Various departments have been organised to look after house maintenance, furniture, electricity, plumbing, sanitation etc. Clothing is made by two tailoring departments and regular laundry service is provided by the "Blanchisserie". A shoemaking department and a weaving department supply other necessities. The department called "Prosperity" looks after the storage and distribution of these goods. Inmates indicate their monthly requirements on special forms and receive them from Prosperity on the first of the month.

At the common kitchen, food for 2000 persons is prepared three times a day. Rice, vegetables and fruits are grown in various farms, fields and gardens belonging to the Ashram. A separate kitchen called "Corner House" is run for the students and teachers of the Centre of Education.

Medical care is available at various clinics staffed by physicians of the allopathic, homoeopathic, ayurvedic and naturopathic systems. There is also a dental section, an eye clinic, and a department specialising in physiotherapy, massage and acupuncture.

The Reception Service looks after the needs of visitors and arranges accommodation for them in the Ashram's guest houses.

The Ashram fosters a variety of artistic and cultural activities. There is a theatre for dramatic and other performances, an art gallery, a studio for painting and sculpture, a dance hall and a music room where both Indian and Western music is played. The Ashram's large library is utilised both by students of the Centre of Education and by Ashram members, a number of whom are involved in literary activities and research. A separate Archives and Research Library has been established to preserve the manuscripts of Sri Aurobindo and the Mother to prepare material for publication.

Numerous books and journals have been printed at the Sri Aurobindo Ashram Press since 1945. Recently other printing units have been added to meet an increased production demand. The Press is only one of a number of small-scale industries that have grown up around the Ashram. These units are governed by a separate trust, the benefits of which are donated to the Ashram Trust. Some of the industries represented are woodworking, stainless steel fabrication, handmade paper manufacture, and such cottage industries as the making of handicrafts and incense, and the hand-marbling of silk fabrics. Smaller sections produce embroidered goods, perfume, pottery, batik work, etc.

The Sri Aurobindo Ashram is administered by the Sri Aurobindo Ashram Trust, a public charitable trust managed by a board of five trustees, most of whom were appointed by the Mother. The Centre of Education is an intrinsic part of the Trust.

The Ashram is supported by the devotees and admirers of Sri Aurobindo and the Mother. Recently it "has been approved by Indian Council of Medical Research, the prescribed authority, for the purpose of clause (ii) of sub-section (I) of Section 35 of the Income Tax Act, 1961, for Research purposes only." Therefore any sum paid to the Sri Aurobindo Ashram by assessees assessable under the head "business of profession" is entirely deductible from the total income, provided the payment is for the scientific research purposes of the Ashram. The mention that the payment is for scientific research purposes is essential.

The Ashram is also exempted under Section 88 (at present Section 80-G) of the Income Tax Act, 1961. Consequently donors of all other categories will benefit of "deduction" in accordance with the provisions of this Section.

SRI AUROBINDO INTERNATIONAL CENTRE OF EDUCATION

Before the 1940s children were, as a rule, not permitted to live in the Ashram. But when, during the war, a number of families were admitted, it was found necessary to initiate a course of instruction for the children. Accordingly, on 2 December 1943 the Mother opened a school for about twenty pupils. She herself was one of the teachers. The number of children increased gradually over the next seven years.

On 24 April 1951 the Mother presided over a convention where it was resolved to establish an "international university centre", and on 6 January 1952 she inaugurated the Sri Aurobindo International University Centre. The name of this institution was changed in 1959 to the Sri Aurobindo International Centre of Education.

At present, the Centre of Education has about 150 full or part time teachers and 450 students, ranging from nursery to advanced levels. The curriculum includes the humanities, languages, fine arts, sciences, engineering, technology and vocational training. Facilities include libraries, laboratories, workshops, a theatre and studios for dance, music, painting, etc.

The Centre of Education seeks to develop every aspect of the child, rather than to concentrate exclusively on mental training. A special emphasis is put on physical education. All students (as well as many Ashram members) take part in daily physical activities, including athletics, aquatics, gymnastics, games, combative sports and asanas. The department of physical education maintains a fully equipped sportsground, a swimming pool, a recently built gymnasium, tennis courts, a judo hall, a playground and other modern facilities.

Instruction at the Centre of Education is given according to the "free progress system", which is, in the words of the Mother, "a progress guided by the soul and not subject to habits, conventions or preconceived ideas". The student is encouraged to learn by himself, choose his own subjects of study, progress at a pace suited to his own needs and ultimately to take charge over his development. The teacher is more an adviser and source of information than an instructor. In practice, this system is adapted to the temperament of teacher and student, and some still prefer traditional methods utilising prescribed courses of study with direct instruction by the teacher.

Sciences and mathematics are studied in French, other subjects in English. Each student is encouraged to learn his mother-tongue and Sanskrit, and some study additional languages, both Indian and European.

The Centre of Education does not award degrees or diplomas, since it seeks to awaken in its students the joy of learning and an aspiration for progress independent of outer motives.

WORKS OF SRI AUROBINDO

YOGA

Bases of Yoga
The Four Aids
Letters on Yoga (in three volumes)
Lights on Yoga
More Lights on Yoga
The Mother
The Synthesis of Yoga
The Yoga and Its Objects

PHILOSOPHY

Evolution
Essays Divine and Human
Heraclitus
The Hour of God
Ideal and Progress
The Life Divine
The Problem of Rebirth
The Riddle of this World
The Superman
The Supramental Manifestation and Other Writings
The Supramental Manifestation Upon Earth
Thoughts and Aphorisms
Thoughts and Glimpses

VEDA – UPANISHADS – GITA

Essays on the Gita
Hymns to the Mystic Fire
Isha Upanishad
On the Mahabharata
On the Veda
The Philosophy of the Upanishads

The Secret of the Veda
Sriaravindopanishad
The Upanishads

INDIAN NATIONALISM – INDIAN CULTURE

Bande Mataram
Bankim Chandra Chatterjee
Bankim – Tilak – Dayanand
The Brain of India
The Chariot of Jagannath
Hymn to Durga
The Foundations of Indian Culture
The Ideal of the Karmayogin
The National Value of Art
The Renaissance in India
Speeches
Tales of Prison Life
Uttarpara Speech

SOCIAL AND POLITICAL THOUGHT

The Human Cycle, The Ideal of Human Unity, and War and
Self-Determination

POETRY

Baji Prabhou
Collected Poems
Ilion
Love and Death
Sonnets
Savitri
Supplement to the Revised Edition of Savitri

DRAMA

Collected Plays and Short Stories
Eric
Perseus the Deliverer
Rodogune

LITERATURE

Conversations of the Dead
The Future Poetry
Letters on Poetry, Literature and Art
Letters on "Savitri"
The Phantom Hour and Other Stories
Views and Reviews

TRANSLATIONS

The Century of Life
Songs of Vidyapati

AUTOBIOGRAPHICAL

Sri Aurobindo on Himself

GLOSSARY AND INDEX

Glossary and Index of Proper Names in Sri Aurobindo's
    Works
Glossary of Terms in Sri Aurobindo's Writings

The complete works of Sri Aurobindo are being issued in a new uniform edition of 35 volumes to commemorate the 125th Birth Anniversary of Sri Aurobindo. Subscription to this set is available at a special pre-publication rate, and readers may subscribe to this set and obtain volumes as they come out in batches of 3 volumes.

WORKS OF THE MOTHER

About Savitri
Burning Brazier
Commentaries on the Dhammapada
Commentaries on "Elements of Yoga"
Commentaries on "The Life Divine"
Conversations 1929, 30-31
Flowers and their Messages
Guidance in work
Health and Healing in Yoga
Ideal Child
On Education
The Lesson of Life
The Mother on Herself
More Answers from the Mother
Notes on the Way
On Thoughts and Aphorisms
Paintings and Drawings
Prayers and Meditations
Questions and Answers 1953
Rays of Light
Some Answers from the Mother
The Supreme Discovery
The Sunlit Path
Tales of all Times
White Roses
Words of Long Ago